A Gift For:

_____

From:

_____

Published in 2012 by Hallmark Gift Books,
a division of Hallmark Cards, Inc.,
under license from Random House Publishing
Kansas City, MO 64141
Visit us on the Web at www.Hallmark.com.

Art Director: Chris Opheim
Designer and Production Artist: Dan Horton

ISBN: 978-1-59530-498-8
BOK4159

Printed and bound in China
JAN12

All I Really Need to Know I Learned in

Kindergarten

Robert Fulghum

All I really need to know

about how to live

and what to do

and how to be

I learned in **kindergarten.**

Wisdom was not at the top

of the graduate-school mountain,

but there in the sandpile

at Sunday School.

These are the things I learned:

Share everything.

Play fair.

Don't hit people.

Put things back where you found them.

Clean up your own mess.

Don't take things that aren't yours.

Say sorry when you hurt somebody.

Wash your hands before you eat.

Flush.

Warm cookies and milk are good for you.

Live a balanced life—

learn some and think some

and draw

and paint

and sing

and dance

and play

and work every day some.

Take a nap every afternoon.

When you go out into the world,

watch out for traffic,
hold hands,
and stick together.

Wonder.

Remember the little seed

in the Styrofoam cup:

The roots go down

and the plant goes up

and nobody really knows

how or why,

but we are **all** like this.

Goldfish

and hamsters

and white mice

and even the little seed

in the Styrofoam cup—

they all die.

So do we.

And then remember

the Dick-and-Jane books

and the first word

you learned—

the **biggest** word of all—

LOOK.

Everything
you need to know
is in there
somewhere.

The Golden Rule

and **love**

and basic sanitation.

Ecology and politics

and equality

and **sane living.**

Take any one of those items

and extrapolate it

into sophisticated adult terms

and apply it to your family life

or your work or your government

or your world

**and it holds true
and clear
and firm.**

Think what a better world

it would be if we all

—the whole world—

had cookies and milk at

about three o'clock

every afternoon and then

lay down with blankies for a nap.

Or if all governments

had as a basic policy

to always put things back

where they found them

and to clean up

their own mess.

And it is still true,

no matter how old you are—when

you go out into the world,

it is best

to hold hands

and stick together.